The Journey from Doubt to Faith

Joseph Eugene Young

PublishAmerica
Baltimore

© 2012 by Joseph Eugene Young.
All rights reserved. No part of this book may be reproduced, stored in a retrieval system or transmitted in any form or by any means without the prior written permission of the publishers, except by a reviewer who may quote brief passages in a review to be printed in a newspaper, magazine or journal.

First printing

PublishAmerica has allowed this work to remain exactly as the author intended, verbatim, without editorial input.

Hardcover 9781462661121
PUBLISHED BY PUBLISHAMERICA, LLLP
www.publishamerica.com
Baltimore

Printed in the United States of America

*Dedicated to my only so*n
Daniel Eugene Young
Whose encouragement motivated me
to get this book published

"A wise son brings joy to his father"
Proverbs 10:1

Contents

INTRODUCTION 5

1. IS THERE A GOD? 9
2. IS THE BIBLE AUTHENTIC? 12
3. MUST EVERYONE BE BORN AGAIN? 17
4. DID CHRIST REALLY DIE FOR MY SINS? 23
5. DID JESUS REALLY RISE FROM THE DEAD? 28
6. DID THE VIRGIN BIRTH REALLY OCCUR? 32
7. WILL THERE BE A SECOND COMING OF CHRIST? ... 35
8. WHY ARE THERE NATURAL DISASTERS AND EVIL? ... 40
9. IS THERE A DEVIL? 45
10. IS THERE A HELL? 49
11. ARE THERE ANGELS? 54
12. DO MIRACLES REALLY HAPPEN? 57
13. ARE PRAYERS REALLY ANSWERED? 62
14. IS THERE LIFE AFTER DEATH? 70

EPILOGUE 75
APPENDIX 76

INTRODUCTION

Our first Christian beliefs may come from our parents, the church, the Sunday School, our peers or possibly from our own study. But before we live very long we begin to question whether those beliefs are true. Doubts begin to form in our mind and we become uncertain if some of our handed down beliefs are valid.

The method for dealing with doubt was aptly expressed by Rudyard Kipling in his poem, "The Elephant's Child."

> "I keep six honest-serving men
> (They taught me all I knew);
> Their names are What and Why And When
> And How and Where and Who."

Raising questions about beliefs is the process whereby our doubts can be changed. Either we will reject, adopt, or modify beliefs when we allow these "six honest servingmen" to address them.

Some supposedly Christian groups regard doubt as a sin. This book is based on an alternate view that doubt is an important ingredient in Christian growth. When we doubt a belief we ask why the belief is essential; we inquire about its origin; we study to see what beneficial effect it has had in history; we look at the lives of people who have held the belief; and we consider how it would creatively change our life.

Eventually we begin to doubt some of our doubts. Then because we have thought through our beliefs they become our own. Doubts may well be the means by which our beliefs become well defined. Doubts may cause us to check our thinking with other Christians. Doubt is one of God's most effective tools for producing a workable faith.

So, it is not unreasonable to raise some doubts concerning our beliefs. Indeed thinking persons can do no less. I believe Christians will not be cast out for raising doubts. More likely they will be judged for glibly accepting beliefs without examining them carefully.

We will never be able to increase our faith by ignoring doubt. Rather it is doubt that finally enables faith to bloom.

Once we have cultivated our own beliefs by careful thought and thorough examination, then our beliefs can flower and add beauty to our lives and the world in which we live.

Beliefs provide our "reason to be" and give direction to our living. Jesus never required acceptance of any theological statement to be a follower. Rather he asked us to love God and to love our neighbor as ourselves. So let's address our doubts and work through them to a valid and practical belief. I hope this book will help you in that very personal process.

If you would like to use this book in a study group you will find questions for discussion in the appendix.

CHAPTER 1
IS THERE A GOD?

Do you doubt the existence of God? Certainly no one is going to prove God's existence. You cannot conduct a scientific experiment in a test tube that will materialize divinity.

However, there are several important consideration that have minimized my doubts.

Back in 1950 I was a college student at Simpson College, Indianola, Iowa. Under the guidance of a professor we began to study the structure of matter. We were taught that matter is made up of molecules containing atoms, and within each atom there is a nucleus with protons and electrons in orbit around it. This was like a miniature solar system.

Then our study moved from the minuscule atom to the mammoth galaxies. When we see the dense stars in the night sky that we call the Milky Way it is because we are looking longitudinally through our own galaxy, that has a diameter of 100,000 light years. Our galaxy is in a spiral, with our solar system in orbit around the denser cluster of stars in the center of the system.

Then one day it dawned on me that this universe is no accident. It is the work of a designing mind. There is a similar pattern from the smallest to the largest: the rotating galaxy, our solar system, and the interior of the atom. One organizing principle runs through it all and my belief in God was strengthened. It was a unifying insight that reinforced my belief.

Yes I could doubt God's existence, but it made more sense for me to believe than to doubt.

When I contemplate the eons of time it has taken for people to evolve; when I consider how the conditions had to be just right for life to be created and sustained; then I can't help but agree with the philosopher who said that the chance of the universe coming into being by accident are about the same as getting Webster's unabridged dictionary as the result of an explosion in a print shop.

Think of the love and care that our mothers and fathers have lavished upon us. Remember how they have nurtured, guided, sacrificed and prayed for us. Consider the time taken to learn, to grow, to begin to care, to love, to develop character.

We spend a lifetime learning to be patient, to be considerate, to be peaceable, to look for the good in others, to forgive.

Does it seem like common sense or justice that all the good we have nurtured will be buried by this experience we call death? I doubt that God would create people to grow and love and then snuff them out like a candle.

I'm keenly aware that nothing I have said proves God's

existence, but nothing anyone else can say disproves it either.

Each of us has to personally decide whether or not we are going to believe. My hope for you is that when common sense motivates you to believe; or when you are seeing the world with a sense of awe and your mind asserts there must be something that survives the grave; that you will turn from doubt and take a leap of faith. It is a good time to decide you are going to live "as if" there is a God. That is an act of faith. When you step out in faith, you will become increasingly convinced that God is with you.

I invite you to place you faith in God. Read the Gospels and start obeying the great truths you find there. Try Jesus' way of ministering to the needs of others; His way of praying for those who abuse us; His way of looking for and affirming the good in others; and His way of loving God and neighbor and self. I believe you will find it to be a most practical and meaningful way to live.

CHAPTER 2
IS THE BIBLE AUTHENTIC?

The Bible is a timeless library of truths about God, but it is not infallible as literalists insist. Very few persons, except arch fundamentalists, believe every word came in on some celestial teletype. Contrary to Old Testament admonitions, even literalists eat pork and put their money out at interest.

However, those who insist that every word is from God hold on to their outmoded beliefs with tenacity. Back in the late 1950s when I was in graduate school there was a group of Zionists north of Chicago who still insisted that the world was flat on the basis of Isaiah's statement that referred to the four corners of the earth (Isaiah 11:12). Even when they were shown pictures taken from a rocket that showed the curvature of the earth's surface, they held to their mistaken belief.

I've always appreciated an illustration once used by Bishop F. Gerald Ensley in which he compared the Bible to a banana. He said the literalist comes to the banana and without peeling it takes a taste. The skin seems tough and insipid, but he says you can't eat just part of it, so he eats it skin and all. The modernist comes to the banana and upon tasting the skin says I can't believe this can be good and throws the whole thing away. The sensible Christian comes to the banana, peels it and eats the edible part. There are too many fundamentalists who say if you are going to believe a part of the Bible you must take it all. Only a fool would conclude there is nothing good there and dispose of all of it. The thoughtful Christians need a way to determine which parts of the Bible truly reveal God and which do not.

I believe Jesus Christ is the key.

Most Christian people have long ago given up on literalism, however, many do doubt that the Old Testament gives a true account of what God is like. The angry, jealous God portrayed in parts of the Old Testament seems far removed from the loving, gracious being we see revealed in Jesus. The Old Testament speaks of God destroying enemies by the sword and I suspect such statements tell us more about the writer's view of history than they tell us about the nature of God. We need a reliable method of sorting out the authentic Word from God, from that which is merely human interpretation.

I believe it is helpful to take Jesus' view of the Bible. He says: "You have heard that it was said, 'An eye for an eye and a tooth for a tooth.' But I say to you, do not resist an evildoer. But if anyone strikes you on the right cheek, turn the other also; and if anyone wants to sue you and take your coat, give your cloak as well; and if anyone forces you to go one mile, go also the second mile." (Matt. 5:38)

Jesus took the Old Testament law and introduced a higher ethic. Jesus had a high regard for the prophets and obviously believed many of their lofty teachings and so held the Bible of his time in high regard, but when he felt it was wrong he did not hesitate to follow a higher authority. We would do well to adopt Jesus' view of the Bible.

The perfect Word, is Jesus Christ. "And the Word became flesh and lived among us, and we have seen his glory, the glory as of a father's only son, full of grace and truth." (John 1:14)

Martin Luther said that too often we have made the Bible into a "paper pope." He explained that the Bible is the cradle that holds the Christ. We do well to regard Jesus as the highest revelation of God's true nature. When we encounter other ideas, whether they are in the Bible or elsewhere, we do well to hold them up to the light of Christ's life and teaching. If they do not measure up to the high standard we see in his life then we should have no qualms about dismissing them.

Be assured there is much in the Old Testament that is consistent with the life and teaching of Jesus. The Old Testament reveals a growing understanding of God. It sets forth the history of the people of Israel and how they grew in understanding of what God required of them. It gives us the teaching of prophets whose message called people to return to the ways of God. Jesus' teachings are clearly grounded in much of their wisdom. It gives us the songs of praise that were doubtless used in their early worship experiences.

Don't allow your doubts to keep you from reading the Bible. It is not an easy book to read but the benefits can equip one for a really good life. There are some parts of the Bible that glow with inspiration (like the 23rd Psalm, the Sermon on the Mount and I Cor. 13); but there are other parts that must be thoughtfully researched and studied before they will yield their treasure. This is a book through which God speaks and His Word to us is clearest when we are focusing upon Jesus Christ.

The great value for us in reading the Bible is the way in which it can enable us to know God, to grow to love God and to find guidance for the daily living of life. If we approach the Scriptures prayerfully, we will be inspired by reading it. That is why people say God's Spirit breathes through the Bible. The Bible lifts our mind and spirit so that we respond creatively to truth, beauty, and goodness—that is why it is inspired.

Most of us are not Bible scholars, but we long to read the Bible and absorb its messages. So start with the Gospels (probably Mark since it was the first one written); use a good modern translation; approach your reading with a prayer indicating your willingness to be open minded; look up key words in a Bible dictionary;

read until an idea leaps up off the page and grabs your mind; and then meditate upon its meaning for your life.

None of us will understand everything in the Bible. There will be a few ideas we doubt, and there will occasionally be an outmoded concept of God we will reject, but there will be ample inspiration to richly reward our investment of time and study.

CHAPTER 3
MUST EVERYONE BE BORN AGAIN?

Arrogance is unattractive wherever it is found. It may be young people holding up their index finger at a ball game and shouting "We're number one," or it may be an adult who refuses to listen and discuss an issue because they think they already have the final word.

There is also a theological arrogance that professes to have God figured out. Whenever you find someone who dogmatically asserts they know the only path to heaven you can be sure you have stumbled into a person whose God is too small.

One of the most offensive forms of Christianity is the self-righteous assertion that "Christ is the only name under heaven whereby you can be saved." Now of course one can find wholeness (salvation) through faith in Christ, but to haughtily contend that Christ is the only road to God implies a denial of every other major religion—including Judaism where we have our roots. Such an overbearing dogmatism is inconsistent with the spirit and teaching of Jesus Christ who extended grace and love to every person and went looking for the lost sheep.

When Jesus said to Nicodemus you must be "born from above" was he talking to you and me as well? Nicodemus was a Pharisee, so consider the "You" in Jesus' statement,

"You must be born from above." (John 3:7) The "You" in the Greek is plural and so some scholars think Jesus may have been referring to the Pharisees as a group. We may be taking undue license with the scripture when we conclude the phrase refers to everybody? It may or it may not.

Some people come to faith in Christ because of some emotional, climactic experience. It might be the response to preaching, it might be an encounter with a terminal illness, it might be a "close call" accident, or it might be some other personal crisis. Like a physical birth that takes place at a specific time and place, that person can point to an event in their history where faith became a reality for them. They may well refer to that personal event as the time when they were "born again."

Other people who are genuinely Christian can't remember when or where they came to faith. They are like Paul's description of Timothy being nurtured at his mother's and grandmother's knee. (II Timothy 1:5) Some people are raised in homes where they are surrounded by positive Christian influences and they gradually grow in faith. They find it difficult to point to any one time and place where they first accepted Christ and were "born again."

Horses are broken to ride in different ways. In the old West, a wild horse would be captured and crowded into the corner of the corral with gates. Then some brave cowboy would climb on and he either got bucked off or he would stay on the horse until its spirit was broken. You could say that on a particular day in that corral the horse was broken to ride. Other horses (usually thorough-bred race horses) at an early age would be led around with a halter. Later a blanket would be placed across their back and they were led around some more. Then a saddle is placed on their back and some weight is gradually put in the saddle. Finally, someone mounts the horse and while there may be some reaction from the horse he/she doesn't buck. Coming to faith is often a gradual experience.

However one becomes a Christian we should rejoice and certainly we should never disparage or "put down" people whose experience is different from ours.

So how ought we react to those persons who ask us if we are saved? When we reply, "Yes, I think so," they respond "If you were saved you would know it." I believe such people have confused faith and knowledge. The latter refers to something that one knows. Faith refers to something one believes with such firmness they are willing to act upon it. The Christian is a person who has committed their life to the belief that God's nature is revealed in Jesus Christ and they have determined to think and act "as if" that is a fact (though they cannot prove it in any scientific sense).

The Christian above all should be intellectually honest. We shouldn't tell others we know something for positive when it is a matter of faith. We should say it is our firm conviction and we are willing to stake our life on its validity. We can say we are persuaded that we have found salvation in Christ, but we shouldn't try to convince someone we have knowledge we really don't possess.

Faith is the hallmark of the Christian. It is faith that keeps us focused forward and growing in Christ likeness. Faith is a trust that God is present and that God loves us, accepts us, and wants that which is best for us. My favorite definition of faith is "betting your life on God." Faith is not a blind leap in the dark.

Faith is going as far as we can with knowledge and experience and then taking a leap in the direction of the greatest probability. Faith is the most sensible of the alternatives we have in life for it is acting upon that which we believe to be the most reasonable and persuasive conviction.

If you didn't know how to swim, you could sit on the edge of the pool and read a manual that would tell you how to move your arms and kick your feet, but you will never learn to swim unless you get in the water and act "as if" you know how to swim. The same could be said for learning to ride a bicycle. Faith is deciding that we will begin to act "as if" God is with us in every aspect of our living. Faith is the result of a personal commitment to invite the presence of God into your life. You can call that "being born again" or you can simply call it "life in

Christ."

It is the essence of what it means to be a Christian. It is Christ in us.

This process of being saved is called salvation. It is being saved from guilt, anxiety, fear, and selfishness. It is being saved to forgiveness, peace, joy, love, kindness, and goodness. One doesn't suddenly become perfect, but one has a new outlook, and a new perspective. When a person is saved they feel secure in God's presence. "If God be for us who can be against us?" said Paul. (Romans 8:31) Even in the face of death the Christian holds firm to the conviction that God will take care of them.

"Yea, though I walk through the valley of the shadow of death, I will fear no evil, for Thou art with me." (Psalm 23:4)

Salvation is a process that is due to God's Grace. It has been described by saying that God reaches down with his hand (Grace), and people reach up with their hands (faith), and salvation is the result. God's action in Christ and our response of trust brings the Holy Spirit into our lives.

Now with that background I can say that I believe I have been "born again." When I was a senior in high school we had revival services at our church. I listened to the preacher each night and I had a sense of guilt for the things I had done wrong.

Actually I had not committed any heinous crimes but I had not been right in my relationships with others and so I responded to the minister's invitation to come to the altar and give my life to Christ. When I finally knelt at the altar and asked God's forgiveness something great happened in my life. I did feel that God forgave me and a great sense of purpose flooded over me. I felt that a great load had been lifted from me and now I knew what I was to do with my life.

The emotional high from that experience lasted two or three weeks, but yet to this day I know it was a time that I took a significant step toward God in my living. Through the years I have conversed with scores of people about how they came to have faith in Christ. The experiences are very diverse and all of them are authentic. People come to faith in as many different ways as there are people. Let us be thankful that our God is a mysterious and creative God who is so much bigger and wonderful than anything we can imagine and that God reveals Him/Herself to us in a multitude of exciting and profound ways and experiences.

CHAPTER 4
DID CHRIST REALLY DIE FOR MY SINS?

Could it be that Jesus, who died 2000 years before me, can actually save me from the consequences of all the things I've done wrong? Pardon my doubt, but the idea seems preposterous. Yet when I ask the average Christian what Christ has done for them they mouth the cliché "Christ died for my sins?" But when I ask them to explain what that means or how that can be, the answer doesn't come easily.

Let's think first about some of the ideas or theories that have been traditionally given.

The early church held to the "Ransom Theory." This concept was that the suffering and death of Jesus was a ransom God had to pay to the devil so he would let humankind out of his clutch. In the contemporary Greek thought a ransom was the money a person paid to free a slave. It is this theory that is behind the statement often heard that "Jesus paid the price for our sins." This is a strained argument for I doubt that God negotiates with the powers of darkness. Further, if my child is disobedient I do not require that some innocent person must suffer before I can forgive my child, surely God can forgive without having to require the crucifixion of His beloved Son.

Another ancient theory of the atonement sees God as the universal Judge. Since we have disobeyed God's law, if God is to be just, we must be punished (Penal Theory). So Christ takes the punishment for us and thereby God's justice is satisfied and we are then accepted by God. Surely God would not inflict punishment upon one who had lived an exemplary life and who was innocent of any wrong doing. What kind of justice is that?

Why punish a person like Jesus for what I have done wrong 2000 years later?

Still another view of the atonement portrays Jesus as the sacrificial lamb that must be slain in order to appease God's anger toward our sin (Satisfaction Theory). Clearly this concept had its roots in early Jewish thinking. The Old Testament book of Leviticus sets forth a myriad of regulations concerning how sacrifices are to be made. It was the common belief that a sacrifice on the altar was necessary to atone for sin and win God's favor. Also the mystery religions of the day required the sacrifice of an animal. The blood was then poured over the initiate to appease the anger of the wrathful God. However the worshiper in the pew today can easily do without the imagery about being "washed in the blood of the Lamb." You would think the church by this time ought to have progressed beyond the mystery religions. Especially if we would have taken to heart the words of the Prophet Hosea who portrayed God as saying "For I desire steadfast love and not sacrifice, the knowledge of God rather than burnt offerings." (Hosea 6:6) Or consider the Psalmist who said: "For you have no delight in sacrifice; if I were to give a burnt offering you would not be pleased. The sacrifice acceptable to God is a broken spirit; a broken and contrite heart O God, you will not despise." (Psalm 51:16-17)

My doubting heart requires another view of the cross and what happened there. Jesus could have avoided the cross, but for some reason he chose to endure the intense suffering of a crucifixion. Jesus went to Jerusalem intentionally. He antagonized the temple authorities by casting out the money changers, and even up to the last evening he could have escaped but rather went along with Judas' plot knowing it would result in his arrest. Jesus prayed so intensely about it that he sweat as it were "drops of blood." (Luke 22:44) He was resolutely willing to do his Father's will. I believe the cross was a voluntary decision on Jesus' part. So Jesus was not a helpless captive of Pilate. He was there because he believed his death would convey a crucial truth.

The most powerful statement any human being can make is to be willing to die for what they believe is right and good.

Indeed the highest love is to give your life for another. So Jesus' voluntary acceptance of the crucifixion was a loud and clear declaration that God's love is extended to everyone. Even the thieves beside Jesus felt his acceptance. All those gathered around the cross heard him offer forgiveness to the perpetrators of that ghastly deed.

All of us, even centuries later, when we contemplate Jesus' willingness to give himself, begin to marvel at this incomprehensible love that goes on loving even to the uttermost.

For me, the inescapable conclusion is that God's love was being revealed. Here is the divine love that goes on caring no matter how difficult the circumstance.

Jesus crucifixion is telling me that at the heart of the universe there is a being who loves me to the uttermost. Even though I have sinned God's response to me and to you is to go on loving us, forgiving us, and seeking to lead us to redemption. In a most dynamic way Christ did indeed "die for my (our) sins."

Further, it is astonishing to recognize the relationship between Jesus' sharing the Passover Feast with the disciples and the crucifixion. Recall that Jesus told the disciples that he had longed to share this Passover Feast with them. (Luke 22:15)

Jesus "took a loaf of bread, and when he had given thanks, he broke it and gave it to them, saying, 'This is my body, which is given for you. Do this in remembrance of me.' And he did the same with the cup after supper, saying, 'This cup that is poured out for you is the new covenant in my blood.'" (Luke 22:19-20)

Then he goes to the cross where his body and blood are given in a great act of love. His death on the cross sealed a new covenant in which we may be assured that he is committed to help us become what God intends for us. When we become a Christian we are committed to Jesus, and the cross assures us that He is committed to us. What a privilege it is to be in a covenant relationship with Jesus who can rightly be called our "Lord and Savior."

CHAPTER 5
DID JESUS REALLY RISE FROM THE DEAD?

At the heart of our Christian Faith is the belief in the resurrection of Jesus from the dead. Yet from a human perspective it seems incredible to believe such a phenomenon.

There have been some unusual resuscitations of human beings, but to come back to life after one is physically dead is beyond our understanding, and it ought not surprise anyone that many people doubt that it is true.

Some spiritualize the event and maintain that Jesus didn't physically come back to life after being dead for three days, but that the quality of his life and love while alive was so great that his spiritual presence continues even though his body has decayed somewhere.

Certainly no one can prove that Jesus rose from the grave.

But someway the disciples became so convinced that Jesus was alive that they went out into the world and ultimately gave their lives proclaiming that Jesus was alive and that the resurrection was real. People don't usually give their lives for a lie. For me it is the conduct of the disciples that provides the most salient argument for the resurrection. Their holding to the belief in Jesus' resurrection in the face of persecution and finally martyrdom is the clincher for me. Surely the Jews and the Romans would have produced Jesus' dead body if they could have, for they wanted to stop the spread of Christianity.

Then of course there is the biblical testimony and the recorded appearances of Jesus following the crucifixion. Frank Morrison was a man who set out to prove that the resurrection was a hoax. He studied the biblical stories comparing the different accounts and became convinced of the validity of the resurrection and wrote a book called "Who Moved the Stone?"

Consider a verse from the Gospel of John: "Then the other disciple, who reached the tomb first, also went in, and he saw and believed." (John 20:8) It was early on Sunday morning.

Mary came breathlessly to Peter and John and reported that the body of Jesus was gone from the tomb. They "took off" immediately to see for themselves. Now John was the faster runner and got there first. He looked in and he saw the linen clothes in which Jesus had been wrapped lying there in place.

John must have thought to himself—if someone had stolen or removed Jesus' body, why would they leave the grave clothes?

Then something else registered in his thinking—the grave clothes were not messed up or disheveled, as they would be if someone took them off. They were lying there "still in their folds." The Greek word here implies the grave clothes were in their regular place as if the body of Jesus had simply evaporated out of them and left them lying. The sight quickly penetrated into John's mind; he realized what had happened—and he believed.

The resurrection does seem to be the logical conclusion to the life of this itinerate teacher whose message was astounding and whose quality of life was utterly consistent with his words.

The resurrection is the stamp of God's approval on this perfect life that serves as an example and pattern for all of us.

Since we cannot prove the validity of the resurrection each person has to decide whether to accept it or not. Faith is betting one's life that it is true and making a personal commitment to follow in the way of Jesus. Faith is deciding to live "as if" the resurrection is true and Jesus is present with us. Faith invites his Living Spirit into the very core of our being and that empowers and inspires us toward wholeness.

Life is frequently difficult, filled with problems, suffering or hardships. A lot of people get discouraged and give up on some Calvary hill in their life. But if only we would be patient and keep doing the best we can under the circumstance, we would soon discover that following the crucifixion comes the resurrection. Sure troubles come, but hold onto the belief that spring follows winter, after darkness comes the dawn, and Easter crowns Calvary. This is the heart of the Christian faith.

The cross, which might have been a sign of defeat, has been transformed into a glorious victory by the resurrection. Our faith is one that can look at the evils of the world and still maintain a spirit of optimism because we believe God has overcome sin and death.

As a pastor I have been in a lot of cemeteries and I have seen some impressive graves and tombstones. But the simple tomb given by Joseph of Arimathea for Jesus' burial has a more distinctive feature—there is no one in it. The vacant tomb is central to our faith—"Christ Is Risen."

CHAPTER 6
DID THE VIRGIN BIRTH REALLY OCCUR?

We don't go far in the Gospel narrative until we read about how Jesus was born. Joseph and Mary had plans to be married.

They were in what we would call the engagement period. Mary has a visit from an angel and is told that she has been chosen for a very special assignment and that she will become pregnant by the Holy Spirit. Then before she lives with Joseph she is pregnant.

Now it is possible that Joseph was responsible for her conceiving, and together they might have concocted a story about a virgin birth to divert attention from their lustful, loving adventure. However, that is an unlikely scenario, since why would they make up a story about having a virgin birth and expect people to believe it? Joseph, according to scripture, is an upright and kind man who does not want to publicly disgrace Mary. So Joseph decides to quietly terminate their relationship.

Joseph probably wonders if Mary has been unfaithful to him, but then an angel appears to him and tells him it is a virgin birth. Joseph decided to "hang in there" and see what happens.

Now it ought not to surprise us that there are people who doubt the virgin birth. Of course there are all kinds of bizarre theories—like a sperm from someone's ejaculation in Mary's bath water—but the likelihood of a sperm living in that kind of setting is extremely remote. The unique thing about a virgin birth is that it almost has to be some kind of divine intervention.

Obviously it is not the way things usually happen in the world.

First let's look at the Biblical facts that might relate to whether the virgin birth is true or false. The Gospel of Mark, which was the first Gospel written, doesn't mention it. The Gospel of John, which was the last Gospel written, doesn't mention it either. Only Matthew and Luke refer to the virgin birth. The Apostle Paul, who wrote nearly two-thirds of the New Testament, never alludes to it. Perhaps even more astounding is the realization that Jesus himself never spoke of it. Surely we ought not require belief in something when the founder of our faith never mentioned it. Further, a careful reading of Matthew shows that the author goes to great length (half of the first chapter) tracing the linage of Jesus through Joseph all the way back to Abraham. That would surely be a futile exercise if Joseph were not the father of Jesus.

There is a distinct possibility that it was a doctrine created after the life and death of Jesus. That the early church in their joy and enthusiasm for the Christian life just couldn't believe that Jesus came into existence in a normal way, and so they put together this beautiful story to explain his supernatural origin.

So it ought not surprise us that many cannot swallow the idea of a virgin birth. And most assuredly believing in the virgin birth of Jesus is not a requirement for being a Christian.

(However, there are some sect churches that require the believer to subscribe to a list of doctrines before they can become a member and in such churches belief in a virgin birth is usually on the list.)

Having said all that, I must confess that I do believe in the virgin birth. To me it is a minor miracle when compared to the life-empowering resurrection of Jesus from the tomb. The virgin birth is an appropriate beginning for the life of one who brings the message of the Creator of the universe and who provides a life-transforming power for those who believe.

CHAPTER 7
WILL THERE BE A SECOND COMING OF CHRIST?

Is there going to be a time when Jesus Christ will return to the earth to straighten out the problems in which we find ourselves? Or does he just come and take the Christians out of the world and its troubles? I must confess I have some doubts about the second coming of Christ.

First, let's consider the biblical testimony. The Bible does not use the phrase "second coming" but it does speak numerous times of his appearing in the future. These references have been interpreted in many different ways. For example some believe the second coming happens for each person at the time of their death because on the evening before the crucifixion Jesus said, "In my Father's house there are many dwelling places. If it were not so, would I have told you I go to prepare a place for you? And if I go and prepare a place for you, I will come again and take you to myself, that where I am you may be also."(John 14:2-3)

Still others regard the second coming as the arrival of the Holy Spirit at Pentecost. This is a reasonable assumption because Jesus talked to the disciples about sending them an "Advocate" a "Spirit of truth" to be with them. (John 14:16-17) Then in the next sentence he says "I will not leave you orphaned; I am coming to you." Those who hold this perspective believe the second coming has already occurred.

Still others regard the second coming as the time when Christ first came into their life—the time of their conversion—the time of their decision to be a Christian. Such persons see the second coming as the time that faith dawned in their life.

Appealing as these views may be, when we honestly look at the biblical testimony it is clear that a multitude of references point to a future event in which Christ's coming will be visible to people here on earth. The time of this cosmic event cannot be discerned and so we are advised to be constantly ready.

The first letter by Paul to the church at Thessalonica was one of the earliest that he wrote. Paul had received word from them via Timothy, and while it was a favorable report, Paul wanted to correct their misconception about the second coming of Christ. Paul makes it clear that no one knows when Christ will return and those who are "children of the light" (in Christ) will be saved.

Paul wrote a second letter to the church at Thessalonica soon after the first because apparently some had misinterpreted Paul's comment about the second coming of Christ. Some had reasoned that since Jesus' coming was imminent why should they work, so all they were doing was waiting. Paul again affirms the coming return of Christ but he admonishes them to not listen to rumors about it being real soon. Paul enumerates events that are to happen before Christ's coming. There will be rebellion and lawlessness associated with the power of Satan. In the meantime they are to live the Christ-like life and to not tolerate idleness and busybodies.

In First Corinthians 1:7 Paul briefly encourages those who wait for the second coming, but beyond that Paul seldom mentions it again in his writings. It seems the longer Paul lived the less he wrote about it. It is almost as though when Jesus didn't return as soon as Paul had thought he would, he quite naturally began to say less and less about it.

In Mark 13 Jesus is portrayed as talking about the future. In this chapter there is a mixture of information about the destruction of Jerusalem and the second coming. There is description of great suffering that is to occur and emphasis on the abominable desolation that will result. Some of the things mentioned refer to the destruction of Jerusalem but they are at times interpreted as referring to the second coming. For example, Jesus says, "Truly I tell you, this generation will not pass away until all these things have taken place." If Jesus was referring to the second coming, then he was in error. But Jesus was speaking of the coming destruction of Jerusalem and the temple and that prophecy was fulfilled. There are a number of biblical scholars that indicate we can disregard most of the imagery in this chapter, but we should recognize their basic conviction that Christ will come again. Most modern interpreters of this perplexing chapter believe it is colored by the prevailing view in the early church. These early Christians took the vision of Daniel concerning the coming of the Son of man on the clouds of heaven and applied it to the return of Jesus. (Daniel 7:9-14)

In view of the difficulties even the best scholars have in sorting out what Jesus said about the second coming and what the early church may have portrayed Jesus as saying, I think it is proper to try and "zero in" on the things that were central in Jesus' perspective concerning the closing age. Jesus did not spend a lot of time bewailing the evil of his age and concluding it could be remedied only by God's intervention at the end of time. Quite the contrary while he believed that wholeness for a person was something God gives, people do have a crucial part called repentance. We are not to wait for some future day. We are to become children of God and live by faith and goodwill in the present. Further, Jesus seemed to have little patience with those who were always scanning the skies looking for some sign or calculating times or places when God would intervene. Jesus left this timetable to God and busied himself with the great task of inviting people to enter into the Kingdom of God.

There is a great truth inherent in the doctrine of the second coming. I doubt that we need to accept the biblical imagery associated with the second coming, for most of it was a "hand-me-down" from the Jewish thinking about the end times.

However, we should live each day in such a way that if we were to be killed or if life on the planet were to come to an end in some cosmic tragedy we would be ready to meet our Maker. We must always be aware that we do not know the time when our demise will occur and so each day should be lived with joy and enthusiasm for it might indeed be our last.

CHAPTER 8
WHY ARE THERE NATURAL DISASTERS AND EVIL?

Rattlesnakes and mosquitoes seem so unnecessary. The rationale for floods, tornadoes, earthquakes, hurricanes, tsunamis, volcanoes, lightening storms, forest fires, and avalanches is hard to explain. Why would a loving God create a world in which natural disasters exterminate and maim so many innocent people? Of all the occurrences that create doubt these are the most difficult to reconcile with our belief in a caring Creator.

It may be that God considered eliminating these destructive storms and pesky creatures from the earth and decided against it for some reason that is concealed from us. Perhaps there is no other way to strengthen character and build courage short of placing such difficult obstacles in the path of people.

However, it ought not surprise us that theological doubt seeps into the minds of people when their house has been blown away by a tornado.

Theologians and philosophers call this the problem of evil and they have spilt barrels of ink trying to offer reasonable explanations. Some theologians and philosophers have suggested that God is not all powerful and that there are other natural forces in the universe that even God is struggling to overcome.

If there is any area where one could justifiably be agnostic, it is this matter of whether God is almighty or finite. If a part of nature is beyond God's control then one can believe that God is exerting what power He/She does have against such evils. Then it will seem that God is on the side of people in a sense in which an Omnipotent One is not. The all-powerful God is certainly a God of love, but it is harder for some to believe in Him/Her than in a finite God. Yet there is a great reluctance to believe that God is not the Creator of all in nature. Since this is an irresolvable theological problem I believe this is an area is which agnosticism is justifiable.

Evils that emerge from a person's wrong choices do not cause us to doubt God's power. However some Old Testament writers seem to conclude that natural tragedies are God's punishment or discipline on persons for having made bad moral choices. However if that were really true, then why doesn't the discipline come at the time of the misdeed?

It seems rather clear that often the innocent are the ones who suffer as the result of natural disasters. No one can deny that many of life's hardships produce endurance and courage and character, but also many of life's disasters result in bitterness and even despair. It is one thing for a ship with hundreds of people on board to sink because of the negligence of a captain in hitting an iceberg (a bad choice or ignoring responsibility), and it is another for an ocean liner to be sunk by a tsunamis (a natural disaster). Who is God punishing or disciplining when hundreds of seemingly innocent people are killed?

I believe there is no adequate explanation, no theology sufficient to satisfy our human longing to know why the innocent suffer. Certainly Jesus was aware of the reality of natural disasters, but he offered no rationale for them. All of the great religions of the world have acknowledged the struggle between good and evil. Hinduism refers to it as a tension between illusion and reality; Zoroastrianism sees it as a conflict between light and darkness; Christianity as a contest between Satan and God.

Each religion sees this pull between that which is right and the wrong.

Suppose we were to let our doubt about God run rampant and conclude that there must not be a God, for such a being would not allow the suffering of the innocent. Humanism would be the highest philosophy one could embrace. Most folks would be more apt to "buy into" hedonism believing that we just as well "live it up" before some calamity wipes us out.

Consider another viewpoint. There are many awesome, creative, and beautiful aspects of creation. I affirm that things scientifically true are of God and therefore evolution is probably the best explanation of how things came to be. I prefer to believe that God has been guiding that process and that people are God's crowning achievement. Whether we believe God is infinite or finite, we can take whatever happens to us and turn it into an opportunity to grow in mind and spirit. I do not believe that God uses natural disasters to punish or discipline people, but they can be used as a means to grow mentally and spiritually. I believe God has established the universe so that it operates by orderly natural laws and God doesn't intervene just to "save my neck" if I accidentally drive into the path of an eighteen wheeler or happen to be in the way of a tornado. I don't know why God has made the world as He/She has, but it is here and I'm glad to be a part of it.

There are areas of experience where knowledge, whether medical, scientific, or psychological, is incomplete. The road of life runs right up to the edge of a cliff. It may be the abyss of some terminal illness or some natural disaster and we come to the end of our human knowledge. We can fall into the chasm of despair or we can make a leap of faith. It is precisely at this point that the Christian faith is most helpful. It doesn't explain the world but it gives us the resource to live in it creatively. We can't explain why there are natural disasters and evil, but be of good cheer for we are followers of the One who said, "In the world you have tribulation, but be of good cheer, I have overcome the world." (John 16:33)

Faith is not a blind leap into space. Faith is a leap in the direction that our knowledge points. It is jumping toward the greatest probability. It is being guided by the noblest hypothesis. I believe that God does understand the problem of evil even if I don't. I believe that God is not giving up on the world, but that God loves the world and is working out His/Her will in the world. I want to be a part of that process.

CHAPTER 9
IS THERE A DEVIL?

My father had an old 78 rpm Victrola and one of his records was called "The Two Jailbirds." It was a discussion between two guys in the jail about why they were there. One said; "That was the devil that made you knock that man down." The other replied; "That may have been the devil that made me knock him down, but that jumping on him was my own idea."

I think it has always been difficult, if not impossible, to distinguish in our mind between what is our own thought and what might be the influence of a demonic power. When I try to be intellectually honest, I must admit that I cannot tell whether a bad thought is my own selfishness or an outside evil force.

People who profess to believe there is a devil are usually trying to hold onto the concept because the Bible writers spoke frequently of such a being. And perhaps the strongest argument for the existence of a personal devil is that Jesus seemed to hold that some people were possessed by demons.

Jesus had a forty day tussle in the dessert with the devil as he was wrestling with the direction his ministry should take. Since no one else was there we must conclude that, when Jesus described his personal experience to the disciples, he explained it in terms of an encounter with the devil.

Jesus' temptation was spiritual. Jesus overcame the temptation to use his great gifts for his own comfort (turning stones into bread), or for self display (jumping from the pinnacle of the temple), or to achieve political power (controlling the kingdoms of the world). We all have this struggle over whether to use our life, our talents, and resource for self advantage or whether to serve God and others. There is no compelling reason why we should make Satan a personal demonic being on the basis of Jesus' temptation experience in the desert. It was clearly symbolic in nature. It is in all probability a word picture of the intense personal struggle Jesus had in deciding upon the direction of his ministry.

The theological question that we need to ask is how are we to take the biblical language about demons and the devil, for it is clear that the New Testament writers did believe in the existence of a personal devil. At the very least we should never minimize the existence of evil and the power of wrong choice to rapidly become compulsive when it is repeated. Each person has to decide what spirit they will allow to enter their mind and spirit.

Is there really any advantage to believing in a personal demonic force? If I conclude that much of my wrong behavior is due to the devil in my life, then I have a convenient scapegoat and it helps absolve me from having to face my errant conduct and do something about it.

One of the strong arguments favoring belief in the devil is how bad some criminals are. They do seem possessed. Serial killers, chronic sex offenders and calloused, insensitive dictators all seem to be incapable of constructive change and under the influence of some satanic force. However, wrong conduct can be so consistent and ingrained that a compulsion finally develops that the person seems incapable of breaking.

The origin of demonology seems to reside in man's attempt to explain the evil in the world. In primitive religion when something couldn't be explained as due to the activity of people it was usually attributed to divine intervention whether it was good or bad. As the God concept developed it began to be felt that the things of questionable or immoral nature ought not be blamed on God and so the concept of fallen angels came into being. In the intertestamental book of Enoch (which was written between 200 and 170 b.c.) one can read of the fall of angels and their lust after the women of earth, with the consequent introduction of sinful practices and demonic influences.

There is very little about Satan in the Old Testament. Actually there are only three references that portray Satan as a personal being and the most notable is in Job where Satan is introduced as someone sent by God to test Job. The great prophets apparently felt belief in demons was inconsistent with belief in Jehovah.

In Jesus' day, belief in demons was widespread. In the simple medical diagnosis of the time possession by a demon was the explanation given many diseases, especially cases of mental aberration. Now whether Jesus shared this popular belief is difficult to say, but the method he used in casting out demons can be psychologically justified, since the poor victim himself had no doubt at all that he was possessed and needed to be delivered. Jesus always sought to win the confidence and co-operation of the sufferer and so he went along with their belief in possession.

There are some things that cannot be explained adequately. Why do we have germs, poisonous snakes, viruses, and other organisms that are a threat to our well-being? Could they be instruments of some demonic force? Christ's own attitude cannot be ignored. He seemed to believe in both angels and demons. So I am agnostic about the devil. I really am reluctant to believe he/she is a personal being because I can't see that such a belief will help me be a better person. Quite the contrary, I might blame my bad behavior on the devil instead of assuming personal responsibility for it. However, I must remain open to the possibility that the devil actually exists because of the reality of extreme cases of evil and because of Jesus' language and experience.

CHAPTER 10
IS THERE A HELL?

It ought not surprise us that thinking people have trouble believing that hell is a place of eternal burning fire where God punishes the unrepentant. Our doubts rise up like smoke. An earthly father who punishes his son for disobedience is not so merciless as to scorch his son with fire and especially not forever, so surely the Creator of people on the planet earth would abide by an even higher standard.

I suppose some might argue that belief in a literal fiery hell acts as a deterrent to wrong doing, but I don't think God is the least bit interested in scaring people into right behavior with threats of continuous torture. Certainly anyone who is a Christian out of a motive of fear has missed the glory of the Christian faith.

There are simplistic misconceptions about hell. Through cartoons and humorous conversation, hell is pictured as a burning inferno with a red clad devil dashing around prodding people in appropriate places with a pitchfork. The paintings of the Middle Ages, the writings of John Milton's "Paradise Lost" and of Dante's "The Divine Comedy" also helped sustain these unfortunate, though classical, descriptions about hell.

Modern people have been right to revolt against the

shoddy thinking and irresponsible scholarship of the Biblical literalists. However, we must also recognize that sin does have drastic consequences. Surely the idea of eternal punishment is inconsistent with the love of God as we know God in Jesus Christ, but we stop short of what the Bible has to say if we do not acknowledge that how we live here determines the quality of our future existence. So let's look at what the Bible, and particularly Jesus, had to say about hell.

There are two words in the Bible that can be translated as hell. The first is the Hebrew word "sheol," which is like the Greek word "hades." It means a place of departed souls. It was regarded as underground in a shadowy dark place. Both the righteous and the wicked went there. It was where everyone went when they died. The second word is the one Jesus used. It is found in the New Testament a dozen times and it is always translated as hell. It is the word "Gehenna" which meant "the Valley of Hinnom."

This valley was just south of Jerusalem. It had a bad reputation for Jews because it was the site where foreign gods had been worshiped and human sacrifices had been made. In Jesus' day it was the city dump for Jerusalem where the rubbish and garbage were discarded and a fire burned all the time to consume the trash. Everything that was useless was thrown there. So Jesus describes it as the place where the "worm never dies, and the fire is not quenched." (Mark 9:48)

It is consistent with Jesus' imagery to regard hell as the place where life is wasted. When we waste time, it is gone forever. When we waste our talent it is diminished. When we are poor stewards of our treasure it will never be all it might have been.

Jesus may have also been implying that hell is where things have gotten so bad in a person's life that they shut out God's help. The early church fathers described hell as separation from God. That was the attitude that Jews had toward the Valley of Hinnom. It was that place on earth where the idolatry had been so terrible that God would not hallow the spot. So in the geography of the soul Jesus may have been saying that a person can get so calloused that their conscience is irredeemable.

Let's be very clear about this. Hell is not the place where God abandons people, it is the place where people abandon God. It is not the doctrine that God ceases to love anyone, it is rather the self-centeredness where a person shuts God out.

Hell is the doctrine of the church that reminds us that each of us must choose in our daily life between good and bad. God never forces Him/Herself upon anyone. The latch to the door of eternity is on the inside of the soul. The doctrine of hell reminds us that we have freedom and that we must choose right from wrong. Hell reminds us that our choices do make a difference.

So what happens to a person when they die? Obviously no living person can answer that question with absolute certainty. We can only answer that question by sharing our faith. I am confident on the basis of Jesus teaching that one's life here does determine the quality of their life after death.

When I die and my soul passes into the spiritual mode, if I have the capacity to appreciate the qualities of Spirit, then I will be in heaven. If I'm bored with the things of God, then I'll be in hell.

The whole purpose of life is that we need to prepare ourselves spiritually in order to be at home in the spiritual world. That doesn't mean that we deny the body and its finer feelings, but it means that we keep focused on the fact that all things physical are to express something spiritual. When we die, material possessions are left behind. Our fame, our earthly position, our social status fall away. We don't suddenly become a perfect saint or a condemned sinner. We will still have the capacity to appreciate or the tendency to denigrate what we developed here on earth.

We will be in heaven or hell depending on our capacity—or lack of it—to enjoy spiritual realities. If we love spiritual qualities here and cultivate them in our relationships then we will be in heaven. But it would be hell to be in a spiritual state and have taste only for things physical. To have the inward desires and appetites of the body but no way to fulfill them would be hell. It is heaven to be able to share ideas and feelings and to enjoy doing so. It is heaven to appreciate love, truth, goodness, kindness, beauty, and character. These kinds of qualities practiced on earth provide a foretaste of the joys of the life after death.

Even if hell is only a spiritual state (and not a literal lake of fire and brimstone) it is still real and ought to give us pause for careful thought. Jesus spoke of it with an earnest urgency: "…if your right hand causes you to sin, cut it off and throw it away; it is better for you to lose one of your members than for your whole body to go into hell." (Matt. 5:30) We have an awesome choice everyday. Remember to choose wisely for ahead of us is a Holy City, but just outside it there is the gruesome city dump.

CHAPTER 11
ARE THERE ANGELS?

In recent years angels have become popular figures in American culture. There have been angel programs on TV, most every craft store has a shelf of them for collectors, and several movies have surfaced featuring human type angels, helping spark a renewal of interest in their existence.

It has also become a word that is frequently used in common parlance, as for example, a particularly cute baby may be referred to as "a little angel." Or someone who does an especially good deed may be referred to as an "angel."

The Bible has a complex angelology. Many of the Biblical references to angels picture them as intermediary beings who seem to be necessary because God is so awesome. It is as though God dwells at an inaccessible height and is surrounded with an impassable barrier of fiery glory. Angels are spiritual beings whose primary function is to display the power and glory of God.

Where heavenly worship is described in the book of Revelation we read that there were "many angels surrounding the throne." (Rev. 5:11) In a time when God was feared in nearly every storm, earthquake, lightening, wind, and flood, God seemed too awesome to approach and so angels were the intermediaries who shielded people from a blinding radiance and glory they would not be able to handle. It is in Christ Jesus that we see the loving side of God's nature, and Jesus taught us to address God as a Father who cares for His/Her children. Thus angels are no longer so necessary to soften our approach to God's greatness and splendor.

A second function of angels was to convey a message. Actually the word angel is a Greek word meaning messenger. There are numerous instances in scripture where an angel brings a message to a human. The best known is probably Gabriel's message to Mary and Joseph, telling that Mary's pregnancy would be by the Holy Spirit. The idea that God sends angels, whether in human form or in a dream or vision, is an interesting and exciting concept. I can only say I have never talked to anyone who claimed to be one. Since there is a long Biblical tradition that speaks of angels I don't think it causes anyone harm if one believes they do exist.

Goodness knows there are times when a guardian angel would be helpful to us. However, since Jesus Christ has helped us realize that God is approachable and because he has brought to us the message about God we need to hear, I don't think a belief in angels is necessary. So personally it is one area where I choose to be agnostic.

It may be that there are angels. Perhaps they have the policy of never revealing that they are an angel. One of the great passages of scripture is Hebrews 13:2 where we read: "Do not neglect to show hospitality to strangers, for thereby some have entertained angels unawares." In this life we will not know whether there are angels or not (unless we are the recipient of a special revelation), but we can't do better than to extend warmth and hospitality to everyone—including strangers who just might be angels.

CHAPTER 12
DO MIRACLES REALLY HAPPEN?

Almost everyone today has a scientific bent in their thinking.

For example, if we see someone walking on water, we don't immediately conclude that it is a miracle. We are more inclined to ask: "Would you mind showing me how you did that?" or "How did you know where the rocks were?" Magicians have so many tricks that seem to defy logic that we are inclined to think almost anything can be done by slight of hand. However, miracles are not acts conjured up by creating an illusion.

Miracles are sometimes defined as an event in history or an occurrence which, on the surface, seems to contradict natural law and therefore is attributed to God. But it doesn't make much sense to believe God created the natural order and then disregards it to accomplish great things. I prefer to believe that miracles take place without defying natural law. It is just that there are many aspects to natural law that we do not yet understand. A miracle is an event or happening in which God's will is done in a way that is beyond our present level of knowledge and ability.

There are numerous miracles recorded in the Old Testament. Among the most memorable are the plagues in Egypt, the parting of the Red Sea, the daily supply of manna in the wilderness journey, and Elijah's successful challenge of the pagan priests of Baal. All of these revealed God's power or His love and care for the people of Israel. Numerous miracles are recorded in the New Testament. There are far too many to list, but we easily recall miracles of healing, dead persons brought back to life, releases from jail, turning water into wine, the powerful spiritual display at Pentecost, Paul's conversion, and greatest of all, the resurrection of Jesus.

It ought not come as a surprise that some doubt the authenticity of miracles. Some of them are hard to swallow and we begin looking for logical explanations. For example, Jesus' feeding of the five thousand is sometimes explained away by indicating that as the people were organized into groups they discovered others had brought some food and then it was shared. Or considering how rapidly storms actually arise and fade away on the Sea of Galilee, Jesus' miracle of calming the sea could have been coincidence. His statement "Peace be still" may have been spoken to the fearful disciples rather than the storm. But the healing miracles can not be easily or quickly dismissed by a simple explanation.

It is clear from the Gospel accounts that what is recorded is only a small fraction of the miracles that were a part of Jesus' ministry. The Gospels record thirty-five miracles in considerable detail, but there were countless others that are only mentioned in passing. In Mark 1:32-33 we read: "That evening at sundown they brought to him all that were sick or possessed by demons. And the whole city was gathered around the door. And he cured many who were sick with various diseases, and cast out many demons; and he would not permit the demons to speak because they knew him." Or consider this experience by the Sea of Galilee: "He told the disciples to have a boat ready for him because of the crowd, so that they would not crush him; for he had cured many, so that all who had diseases pressed upon him to touch him." (Mark 3:9-10) The Gospels present the following as a common occurrence: "And wherever he went, into villages or cities or farms, they laid the sick in the marketplaces, and begged him that they might touch even the fringe of His cloak; and all who touched it were healed." (Mark 6:56)

Jesus' reputation as a healer seemed to be wide spread: "He came down with them and stood on a level place, with a great crowd of his disciples and a multitude of people from all Judea, Jerusalem, and the coast of Tyre and Sidon. They had come to hear him and to be healed of their diseases; and those who were troubled with unclean spirits were cured. And all in the crowd were trying to touch him, for power came out from him and healed all of them." (Luke 6:17-19) Many other similar passages in the Gospels attest to the fact that Jesus' healing ministry was well known and highly effective.

One will always have doubts about the miracles of Jesus until one decides by faith who Jesus is. Once a person concludes that Jesus stands in a special relationship to God and is divine as well as human, then the miracles that express concern and help for needy people are just what you would expect. The most salient argument for Jesus' divinity is not recorded miracles, but the fact that lives are changed by faith in Him.

When biographers write about a great person there is a tendency to exaggerate and embellish. History is full of examples of miracles attributed to great people—often these stories appear after the saint dies. It would be unusual if the Bible did not contain some distortions. It is a scholarly fact that Matthew, who must have had the Gospel of Mark in hand as he wrote, had a tendency to heighten some of the accounts. So it ought not surprise us if some of the miracles attributed to Jesus may not have been miracles at all.

As we deal with our doubts concerning miracles recorded in the Gospels, the best question to ask is not whether this actually happened, but rather is this miracle consistent with the love and compassion that Jesus had for people? I am inclined to believe the healing miracles because they express the deep concern Jesus had for people in need. But turning water into wine, stopping a storm, cursing a fig tree, and directing the disciples where to fish are presented as miracles and they may have been, but they could have been examples of exaggeration or even coincidence. Unless you believe that they show Christ's divinity, nothing important seems to hinge on believing them.

One can be agnostic about such miracles. I don't thing God will put anyone down for that kind of doubt. Indeed God may even applaud it.

In the final analysis, the miracles will not be the deciding factor in convincing anyone today that Jesus was divine. But if one believes that Jesus did stand in a special and unique relationship to God, that he had a special gift from God, that he had unusual powers because of God's Presence in his life, then miracles would be expected and a natural part of His life of love and compassion for others. Jesus himself is the great miracle for he had capabilities and gifts that other people do not have.

So if we believe in the greatest miracle, then the lesser miracles don't have to be explained away.

CHAPTER 13
ARE PRAYERS REALLY ANSWERED?

Are prayers really answered? I have heard farmers pray for rain and I doubted that God would change the climatic conditions because someone was afraid their seed would not germinate. Such rain might aggravate another farmer who has to stop construction on a much needed edifice. But when I looked in the scripture, the Prophet Zechariah says: "Ask rain from the Lord…who gives showers of rain to you." (Zechariah 10:1) The Prophet Zechariah doubtless knows more about it than I do.

We have a long established practice of table grace in our family. But do we really need to remind God to "Bless this food to the needs of our bodies." Aren't the natural processes of nutrition going to take care of that? However, it has unquestionably been a bonding family experience and to this day some of our grandchildren sing table grace in their family.

Consider the Lord's Prayer that too often is said out of habit rather than earnestness. I doubt that any benefit is derived from merely reciting the prayer when we aren't even thinking about what it means. It bothers me when clergy or laity introduce the prayer by saying, "Let us say the Lord's Prayer." Surely if there is anything that distinguishes talking with God from talking to ourselves we should use the words "Let us pray."

Over the years I've had an "on again, off again" prayer life. I would try hard for a while to have a devotional time. I would read scripture and pray and sometimes use a devotional guide. I've used it as time to review goals, plan my day, make lists, and get organized (and there is some value in that); but after a while I'd slip and start diving into the day's work without praying.

A lot of prayers that are offered in public are too general. Life changing prayer needs to be specific and focused on an individual or circumstance. God's Spirit is a quality that is experienced in the inner life. When prayer is centered on a person and their need it seems to help open their mind and feeling to the presence of God. Prayers of healing are often helpful for this very reason.

Even when we pray for a sick person and they get well we must be careful about claiming their healing was due solely to prayer. It may or may not have been. The human body has great curative powers and the person might have gotten well anyway. Further there may have been medicine or other procedures recommended by the doctor that were responsible for the cure. We can express whatever doubt we wish, but if the prayer helped promote the patients mental well being, made their attitude more positive, or even increased their immunity then it was worth the effort.

It is important to always keep uppermost in our minds

the realization that God heals people in many ways, not just through prayer. God also works through medicine, doctors, therapists, supplements, surgery, alternative medicine, and doubtless other channels unknown to people.

Since I have expressed several doubts about prayer, one might have the impression by now that I don't believe in the effectiveness of prayer. But quite the contrary, I believe prayer is a necessary link to God. Recall what Jesus said in the Sermon on the Mount about prayer: "Ask, and it will be given you; seek, and you will find; knock, and it will be opened to you." (Matthew 7:7) Jesus goes on to remind us that just as we will grant the reasonable requests of our children, so God will grant our requests when they are for our good. I trust Jesus that prayer is important.

One of the problems I've had in praying is thinking what to say. When the mind is caught up in deciding what to pray it is probably more a thought exercise than a prayer, for one is not focusing on God. Besides didn't Jesus say: "When you are praying, do not heap up empty phrases as the Gentiles do; for they think that they will be heard because of their many words. Do not be like them, for your Father knows what you need before you ask him." (Matt. 6:7-8)

One possible solution to this wordiness is the practice of Christian meditation. As Christians we have not done much with meditation. We have thought of meditation as thinking a series of ideas or as a sermon or devotional. Eastern cultures and religions have a different and helpful concept of meditation. They see it as a quieting of the mind and spirit that brings relaxation and renewal.

In meditation one doesn't have to wrack the brain trying to say the right thing. Rather the focus is on a single word (or phrase) which keeps the mind focused on the divine source.

Concentrating on breathing is probably the best way of helping the mind focus. There is a close relationship between breath and God. Associating breathing with prayer has been helpful to me. According to the Bible God breathes into us the breathe of life.

As long as we are able to breathe we are alive. One of the great hymns of the church expresses this: "Breathe on me breathe of God, Fill me with life anew." So in Christian meditation one is centering on God's Spirit, inviting His/Her presence into one's life.

Get comfortable and become aware of your breathing. When your mind wanders, bring it back to your breathing. Intentionally breathe deeper than usual from your stomach or diaphragm. As you inhale, concentrate on receiving God's Spirit into your life. Try thinking or saying a word or phrase as you inhale, like "Come Holy Spirit."

This practice is further enhanced by understanding the

physiology of respiration. Focusing on breathing brings stillness to the mind. As you "breathe in," you visualize God's Spirit entering your body. Then as you exhale, visualize that Spirit going to all parts of your body. This symbolism follows the actual process, for when you breathe in oxygen it goes to the lungs. Meanwhile the right side of the heart has received the blood that is returning via the veins after nourishing tissue throughout the body. The right side of the heart then pumps this depleted blood to the lungs where it is filled with new oxygen. Then it returns to the left side of the heart where it is pumped out to nourish the body.

So as you inhale, you are receiving God's life-giving oxygen (and Holy Spirit). Then as you exhale you visualize that loving, healing, divine Spirit going to all parts of your body. Or if you have a problem with a particular part of your body you can visualize the Spirit going there.

When you tire of that repetition then begin intercession You breathe in receiving the Spirit and as you exhale you visualize someone who you believe especially needs God's Spirit. Picture that person in your mind's eye and visualize the Spirit of God entering their body.

Sometimes for variety, instead of focusing on breathing, visualize God as Light. In your mind's eye see yourself enveloped in a pure, white light emanating from God. To the best of your imaginative powers, experience the warmth and love that God is sending to you in that light. Light is a good biblical symbol of God's presence. According to Genesis God brought light into being before people were created. In early worship (as depicted in the Psalms) the Lord was referred to as Light (27:1), and God's word was declared to be a "light" (119:105) to our path. In the New Testament, the Gospel of John tells us that Jesus referred to himself as the "Light of the World."

Light is so mysterious that it makes a tremendous symbol of God. When light goes through a prism it makes all the colors of a rainbow, and humans can only see those frequencies. But just as there are sounds that are too high or low for us to hear—so there are frequencies of light we cannot see. Higher frequencies beyond our vision are X-rays and gamma rays while radio waves and infrared light are frequencies below our vision.

So envisioning God as light, and seeing ourselves bathed in that light is an excellent way to pray without feeling you have to say a lot of words. Then when you want to pray for others just picture them in your mind and bring them into that healing light of God that surrounds you.

In the final analysis, prayer is getting into relationship with God and reaching out to others with that love and grace that God bestows. If traditional ways of praying enable you to do that then rejoice. However, if you have tried making prayers of words and you have found it difficult, then try Christian meditation and let the Spirit flow.

Are prayers really answered? YES. Prayers of thanksgiving are answered by getting us to focus on what God has already done for us, instead of what we don't have. Prayers of praise direct our thought process to the awesome power of God so that we affirm "I can do all things in Christ who strengthens me." (Phil. 4:13) Prayers of confession remove our guilt and replace it with forgiveness and pardon. Prayers of petition (and I have few of these because God has already given me most everything I need) put us in an atmosphere of watchful waiting. Sometimes the answer is "no" or "yes" or "not yet." Prayers of intercession are frequently answered by God granting the request. Keep a written record of the persons for whom you pray and you will see many positive answers. Prayers of listening are often unused, but when we wait in silence for God to suggest something to us, God frequently surfaces an important idea in our thinking. Take that as an answer and act upon the thought. Are prayers really answered? YES and prayer changes one's attitude and life.

Prayer at its best is talking with God as we live throughout the day. I think that is what the Apostle Paul meant by "pray constantly." (1 Thessalonians 5:17) Instead of thinking thoughts to your self, try molding your thought process so you are having a conversation with God. It is not easy and we quickly fall back into our personal monologue—but keep bringing God back into your inner conversation. Meet criticism with "God help me to learn from that." Meet anxiety with "God help me remember the future is in your hands." When someone cuts you off in traffic—instead of calling him/her a name—pray for the person, "God, help that character to begin respecting the rights of other people." When you need to make a decision, ask God for guidance and express your determination to do God's will.

When you find a mess in that public toilet—try to leave the place better than you found it. Be willing to humble yourself—let others go before you. Let your thought process become a dialogue with God. Keep God in your consciousness and you will be surprised by greater joy in your life.

CHAPTER 14
IS THERE LIFE AFTER DEATH?

No one doubts they will eventually die, but many doubt if they will live on after death. Out of the millions of people who have lived, there is no absolute proof that any one of them is still alive in another place. Yet most major religions maintain that the soul continues to live after physical death. It ought not surprise us that some believe death is the end of all personal consciousness. However, there are salient reasons to believe that human beings continue in a spiritual existence.

When one considers the evolutionary progress that people have experienced and the wholesome personality that often takes the better part of a lifetime to develop, it seems illogical to believe that all that love and grace is snuffed out like a candle by death. Immanuel Kant was thinking in the same vein when he indicated it is necessary to have a life beyond this one to balance out the injustices that occur to people here on earth.

Because of the advances made in medical science numerous people have survived "near death" experiences. Many of these people testify to "out of body" happenings in which they saw a beautiful light, heard great music, and seemed to be welcomed to a very pleasant place.

I once visited a college professor in the hospital who

had been resuscitated from heart failure by doctors administering the electric shock to his chest. He told about rising out of his body and was able to see the doctors gathered around him. He saw a beautiful light, heard tremendous music, and said it was a very pleasant experience. Indeed he said it was so neat that when the doctors begin to be successful and he felt himself going back into his body, he felt irritation at the doctors because this great experience was being ended by their treatment. He told me, "If that is what dying is like, I am no longer afraid to die."

In recent years I have read as many accounts as I could find about persons who were clinically dead and then resuscitated.

Most of them were about persons who had died on the operating table and brought back to life or they have been in an accident and revived by paramedics or rescue squads. There are striking similarities in these accounts.

The dying person had a personal consciousness and was aware of what was going on around them even though the persons present thought they were unconscious. Some of them even remembered hearing the words of the doctor pronouncing them dead. The dying felt a great release from pain and suffering, and a great peace and calmness settled over them—greater than they had ever known before.

As they were dying some said they heard a ringing

sound, still others thought it was wind. Others heard majestic music.

Many felt they were being pulled through a tunnel and they experienced being "out of body." They found themselves looking back at their body on the table or where the accident occurred. They were able to describe the treatment that was being done on their body. Perhaps the most astounding note was that these persons experienced no fear. Quite the contrary they felt surrounded by a warm, positive feeling. In some cases they recounted being greeted by family or friends who had died before them.

Most incredible was an indescribable light. It seemed to have an unearthly brilliance and was exceedingly bright, yet it caused no discomfort to the eyes. This light emitted an irresistible magnetic attraction of warmth, acceptance, and peace.

Light is one of the great Biblical symbols for God. The First Letter of John records that "God is light and in Him is no darkness at all." (I John 1:5) Remember the pillar of fire that led the Hebrew people on their journey through the darkness of the wilderness to the promised land. The Psalmist says, "The Lord is my light and my salvation." (27:1) Jesus referred to himself as the "light of the world." (John 8:12) In the light of these "near death" experiences such passages glow in meaning.

I'm aware that these resuscitation experiences

could simply be people's unconscious mind at work in the midst of a crisis. However, it harmonizes with the Biblical testimony and I believe helps confirm that there is something on the other side of death. It helps minimize my doubts.

To those of us who believe that Jesus is our best revelation of God, His testimony concerning life after death is even more important than "near death" experiences. Jesus said: "In my Father's house are many rooms." (John 14:2) Some people have very narrow thoughts about heaven. They think it is just for them and those who think like they do. They want it to be exclusive. Jesus says there are "many rooms."

According to Scripture after death we are given a spiritual body. The Biblical description of Jesus following the resurrection may provide some clues as to the nature of a spiritual body. Jesus was not a ghost or a spirit, for he was able to eat (Luke 24:42). His spiritual body seemed to be able to move through a physical object, for he entered a room where the disciples were together without going through the door. (John 20:19). Since Jesus was readily recognized I would assume that the spiritual body has some of the recognizable features of our physical body. We will recognize people we have known here on earth. I imagine that the things we have learned to appreciate mentally and emotionally here on earth we will still be able to experience in the spiritual state. For example the fruits of the spirit: "love, joy, peace, patience, kindness, goodness, faithfulness, gentleness and self control" (Galatians 5:22) will be readily experienced in a spiritual body.

Remember Jesus' word to the dying thief on the cross, "Today you will be with me in paradise." (Luke 23:43) Jesus spoke with certainty about a life beyond this one.

One of life's greatest mysteries is what happens when we die. In First John we read, "It does not yet appear what we shall be," (3:2) and the Apostle Paul says, "now we see in a mirror dimly, but then face to face." (I Corinthians 13:12) There are some things we cannot know until we have personal experience; however, the testimonies of those who have had "near death" experiences seem to harmonize with the Biblical testimony and that is enough to turn my doubts into faith.

EPILOGUE

Dear Reader,

I pray that your journey from doubt to faith will bring wholeness to your life.

Living by faith brings joy and happiness, rather than the bitterness and gloom of doubt.

The positive outlook of faith keeps one hopeful and eager about the future, instead of the pessimism and fatalism of doubt.

Faith makes room for laughter and loving, instead of the misery and uncertainly of doubt.

Faith leads us to seek the counsel of the Most High, while doubt tends to rebel against God.

Faith engenders gratitude, while doubt says "things always go bad for me."

Faith sees God's Spirit in the circumstances of life, while doubt claims the unusual as mere coincidence.

Faith causes us to break into song, while doubt leaves a sullen silence.

So begin to live "as if" God is with you, remembering that God loves you. Begin to "bet your life on God." Try it—you will be increasingly convinced faith in God is right for you.

Have a Blessed Journey.

APPENDIX

Questions for personal reflection and/or group discussion

CHAPTER 1—IS THERE A GOD?

1. When did you first begin to believe in God? Why?

2. Do you see evidences of God's existence in nature? Explain.

3. Why do you think there might be a designing mind behind the universe?

4. Is evolution a reason to believe or to not believe in God's existence?

5. Does the development of good character and personality cause you to believe in God? Why or why not?

6. Since God's existence cannot be proven, how should we respond to arguments for God's existence?

7. How can we grow in our conviction that there is a God?

8. How would you put the way of Jesus to the test to determine whether or not be believe in God's existence?

CHAPTER 2—IS THE BIBLE AUTHENTIC?

1. What do you believe about the Bible? Is it literally true, word for word? What are some of the things in the Bible that you have trouble taking literally?

2. How does the thoughtful Christian determine which parts of the Bible truly reveal God and which do not? Can you contrast the view of God given in the Old Testament with the view given in the New Testament? How do we sort out the authentic Word from God, from that which is merely human interpretation?

3. What was Jesus' view of the Old Testament?

4. Is it correct to say the Bible is the Word of God? What is the perfect Word?

5. What are some of the teachings of Jesus in the Old Testament that are consistent with His New Testament teachings?

6. What is the value in reading the Bible?

7. What do we mean when we say the Bible is inspired?

8. How should we study the Bible?

CHAPTER 3—MUST EVERYONE BE BORN AGAIN?

1. Give an example of theological arrogance?

2. Is Christ the only way one can come into a relationship with God?

3. When Jesus said to Nicodemus "you must be born again" was he talking to you and me as well?

4. What are some different ways in which persons come to faith in Christ?

5. How ought we react to those persons who ask us "if we are saved?"

6. What is the difference between knowledge and faith?

7. How would you define faith?

8. What happens in a person's life when they accept Christ as their personal savior or when they are "born again?"

9. When a person accepts Christ they are saved "from what" "to what?"

10. What is the relationship between "grace" and "faith?"

11. Share your experience of accepting Christ in your life? How did it happen for you?

CHAPTER 4—DID CHRIST REALLY DIE FOR MY SINS?

1. How would you explain the meaning of the familiar phrase "Christ died for my sins?"

2. Is it necessary for the Son of God to be crucified before God can forgive us of our sins? Why or why not?

3. Is it reasonable for God to require Jesus to be crucified for sins I will commit 2000 years later? Why or why not?

4. Was the sacrifice of Jesus necessary to appease God's anger? Why or why not?

5. Could Jesus have avoided the cross? What are the circumstances that make you think he could have avoided the cross?

6. Does Jesus' voluntary acceptance of the cross say anything about God's love for us and if so what does it say?

7. On the basis of the cross, describe the nature of God's love?

8. How did Jesus establish a new covenant between us and God?

CHAPTER 5—DID JESUS REALLY RISE FROM THE DEAD?

1. Is it necessary to believe in the resurrection to be a Christian?

2. Can one believe in a spiritual (influence) resurrection without affirming a physical resurrection?

3. What to you is the most convincing argument for the physical resurrection of Jesus?

4. When Peter and John looked in the empty tomb, what evidence did they see that Jesus was resurrected (other than the absent body)?

5. In considering the resurrection why is faith essential?

6. Where does a Christian find the motivation to keep on trying?

CHAPTER 6—DID THE VIRGIN BIRTH REALLY OCCUR?

1. When Joseph learned that Mary was pregnant what do you suppose he thought?

2. If you were to make a case against the virgin birth, what reasons would you offer?

3. If Mary had a virgin birth, why does Matthew spend half a chapter tracing Jesus' ancestry through Joseph?

4. Is it necessary to believe in the virgin birth to be a Christian?

5. Why do you believe or not believe in the virgin birth?

CHAPTER 7—WILL THERE BE A SECOND COMING OF CHRIST?

1. What are some of the different interpretations of what the "second coming" means?

2. Why do some Biblical scholars think Paul changed his views concerning the "second coming" as he got older?

3. What effect did belief in the "second coming" have on some of the early Christians?

4. What does Jesus teach concerning the "end times"?

5. What does the "second coming" mean to you?

CHAPTER 8—WHY ARE THERE NATURAL DISASTERS AND EVIL?

1. Can you reconcile natural disasters and the concept of a loving God?

2. Does it help your theological thinking to believe that God is finite? (i.e., does not have control of all of nature.)

3. Do you believe natural disasters are a way of punishing people who have done wrong?

4. What do you believe God is wanting to accomplish in this world? Do natural disasters have a part in His/Her purposes?

5. When natural disasters occur what does faith accomplish?

CHAPTER 9—IS THERE A DEVIL?

1. When I have a bad or evil thought, can I determine whether it is coming from my own selfishness or some demonic power? Why or why not?

2. Why do some people believe there is a personal devil?

3. What did Jesus accomplish in his forty day spiritual struggle in the desert? Have you ever had a similar struggle? Would it be necessary to ascribe such a struggle to the devil?

4. When a person can no longer control their bad behavior and their wrong actions become compulsive, does that mean they are possessed by a demonic force? Why or why not?

5. Why might a belief in demonology develop in primitive religion?

6. Why is there so little about Satan in the Old Testament?

7. Do you think Jesus really shared the popular belief in demons? Why or why not?

8. Can you summarize the arguments for and against belief in a personal devil?

9. Is it all right to be agnostic about belief in a personal devil?

CHAPTER 10—IS THERE A HELL?

1. Do you believe God punishes the unrepentant in an eternal burning fire? Why or why not?

2. Does belief in a hell deter people from wrong conduct? Is fear the method that God uses to induce right behavior?

3. Do you think it is a good idea to envision hell as an inferno with a devil in a red suit with a pitch fork prodding people in appropriate places? What is the origin of such an idea?

4. What are the consequences of sin? Does how we live here determine our eternity?

5. What does the Hebrew word "sheol" mean?

6. Could it be that Jesus regarded hell as the place where life is wasted? Why?

7. Can a person become so calloused that their life is irredeemable?

8. Is hell the place where God abandons people or the place where people abandon God?

9. When we die and our soul passes into the spiritual mode what kind of preparation should we have made to enjoy that existence?

10. What is the reason for physical life?

11. How does the doctrine of hell underscore the importance of choice?

CHAPTER 11—ARE THERE ANGELS?

1. What signs do you see in popular American culture that there is a renewed interest in angels?

2. Does the use of the word "angel" in common parlance always refer to a divine being? Illustrate.

3. Can you recall from Biblical accounts what are the functions of angels?

4. Do you believe God sends angels in human form to help people? Why or why not?

5. Since God has made His message clear in Jesus Christ, do we need to believe in angels anymore? Will God be holding it against me if I choose not to believe in angels?

6. How would you respond to Hebrews 13:2 where we read "Do not neglect to show hospitality to strangers, for thereby some have entertained angels unaware?"

CHAPTER 12—DID THE MIRACLES REALLY HAPPEN?

1. If you saw someone walking on water, what would you think? What would you ask them?

2. How would you define a miracle?

3. Does a miracle defy natural law?

4. What are some of the miracles you can recall from the Old Testament?

5. What are some of the miracles you can recall from the New Testament?

6. Are there some New Testament miracles that might have a rational or coincidental explanation?

7. Are all of Jesus' miracles recorded in the New Testament?

(see Mark 1:32-33, 3:9-10, 6:56, Luke 6:17-19).

8. Could some of the miracles be exaggerations?

9. What are some of the more difficult miracles to believe?

10. What would you regard as the greatest or most significant of all the miracles?

11. Why do you believe in the resurrection of Jesus?

12. What is faith?

13. Do you know of any miracles in your personal life or the life of a close friend or family member?

14. What factors may help a miracle to happen?

CHAPTER 13—ARE PRAYERS REALLY ANSWERED?

1. Do you believe it is proper to pray for a change in weather conditions?

2. Should we keep repeating the same prayer over and over?

3. Is table grace a necessary Christian practice? Won't the natural laws of nutrition apply whether we ask God to "bless this food to the needs of our body" or not?

4. What benefit is derived from reciting the Lord's Prayer?

5. Does prayer seem to you like a "one way" conversation?

6. Have you been able to maintain a consistent daily devotional time? What have you done in devotional times that has been helpful to you?

7. What good is derived from a typical pastoral prayer?

8. What are some of the characteristics of "life changing prayer?"

9. When healing occurs, how does one know it was due to prayer?

10. What are some of the different methods by which people are healed?

11. What is the greatest benefit of prayer?

12. What kind of problems do you have in praying?

13. Is Christian meditation an acceptable form of prayer?

14. How would one go about meditating?

15. In Christian meditation, how would one do intercessory prayer?

CHAPTER 14—IS THERE LIFE AFTER DEATH?

1. What do you believe happens after death and what makes you think so?

2. Can you give a philosophical argument for life after death?

3. What have you heard happens to people who have a "near death" experience?

4. Can you recall instances in the Bible where God is described as "light" or "fire"?

5. Could "near death" experiences simply be the person's unconscious mind at work?

6. What was Jesus' testimony concerning life after death?

7. What do you think the "spiritual body" will be like?

CPSIA information can be obtained at www.ICGtesting.com
Printed in the USA
LVOW041943190212
269361LV00002B/7/P